Sick Sad Stupid You Decide
Tales from the Poison Center

written by

Charisse A. Webb RN

Charisse Webb RN; CSPI

All rights reserved. No part of this book may be reproduced, stored, or transmitted by any means—whether auditory, graphic, mechanical, or electronic—without written permission of both publisher and author, except in the case of brief excerpts used in critical articles and reviews. Unauthorized reproduction of any part of this work is illegal and legally punishable.

The stories in this book depict real-life situations, each of which has been clarified and enriched with the assistance of AI to provide readers with a deeper understanding.

Because of the dynamic nature of the Internet, any web addresses or links contained in this book may have changed since publication and may no longer be valid.

Paperback ISBN-13: 979-8-9895199-0-3
Hardback ISBN-13: 979-8-9895199-1-0
Kindle eBook ISBN-13: 979-8-9895199-2-7
Deluxe Paperback ISBN-13: 979-8-9895199-3-4

Published in the United States of America.

SICK
SAD
Stupid

You Decide

Tales from the POISON CENTER

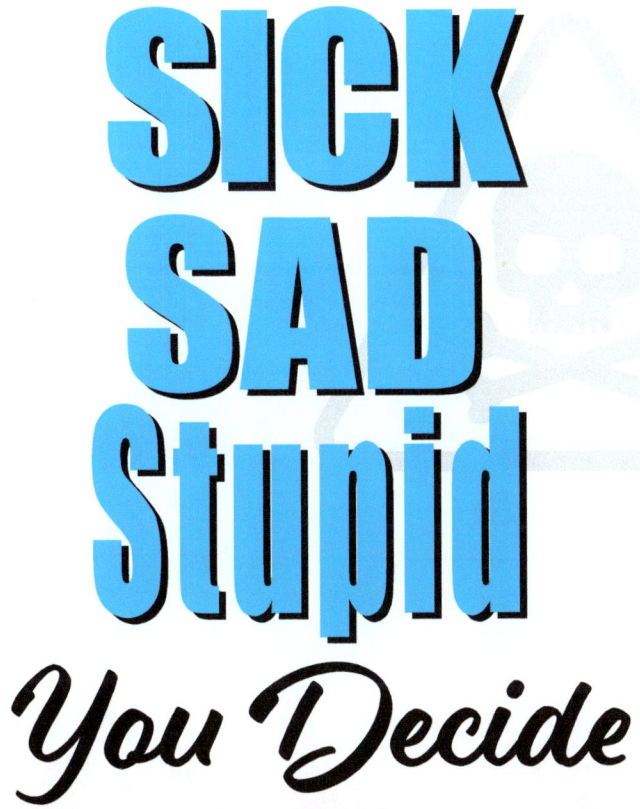

"We make medications in chewable and gummies so kids will eat them.

Frequently if it tastes that good, they will figure out how to get more."

I would like to dedicate this book
to my fellow poison specialists. Your work
is anything but ordinary; it requires a unique
depth and diverse knowledge. Your calm voice at
the end of the Poison Center national telephone number,
giving expert help, makes the world a safer place.

This book is a tribute to the remarkable
contributions of poison specialists worldwide.
Thank you for being the real-life heroes
who light our path in dark times.

Nationwide Emergency Poison Center
800-222-1222

Acknowledgments

I want to thank my family and friends for their understanding and support throughout my career. Choosing a career in healthcare means long hours and irregular shifts. I know I've missed countless important occasions and moments, but your patience and understanding have meant the world to me.

To my healthcare colleagues, I have had the privilege of working alongside some truly amazing individuals. We have spent many days, nights, and holidays together. It has been an honor to share this journey. I am grateful for the everlasting friendships forged with these dedicated people.

Jim Webb, Photojournalist
Betty Norlin, Writing Coach
Susan Blakely, Visual Design
Tom Bostock, Editor

A Special Thank You

I want to especially thank my husband, Jim, for his support and encouragement throughout the challenging journey of writing this book. His belief in me and encouragement kept me motivated during the long hours of writing.

Table of Contents

Dedication 5

Acknowledgments 6

A special thank you to my husband
for his support and encouragement 7

Table of Contents 8

Introduction: 11

Exploring the Path that Led Me to This Moment 12

The History of Poison Center, why do we need them? .. 14

Home Hazards 16

Superglue, Tales from the Sticky side 21

The World of Cleaning products,
the Soap Opera of Spills 22

DIY Mishaps, How to turn do it yourself to DON'T do it .. 24

Sex, Sex & More Sex Quirky Sexcapades 26

Wildlife, Reptile Wrangling, Tales of Scales 28

Insects & Creepy Crawlers
Bloopers of Bug Encounters 32

Marine life, Fishy Fiascos 33

Pesticides, Pest Control Misadventures 34

Plant perils 35

Baby intoxication 36

Suicide 38

Suicide Pacts, Desperate Decisions 44

Culinary Capers, Confessions of a Confused Cook 45

Seasons Eating's, and Festive Follies 47

Beauty Blunders 48

Glamour Mayhem 49

8

Home Remedies, The Cure is Sometimes Worse
Than the Poison: When Healing Hurts. 50

Natural Disasters 52

Matters of Faith, Divine Dilemmas 53

Punishing vs Abuse. 54

Pets, Saliva Showdown of Germs. 55

Sharing Animal Medication 57

Pets With a Bite. 58

Drug Abuse, Mischief in the World of Drug Testing. 59

Happy Hour on the Orthopedic Unit. 60

Running from the Police 64

Mushrooms 64

Forms of Alcohol 65

Addiction 66

Medication Mishaps, Prescriptions Gone Wild. 68

Toy vs Hazards, Child's Play Chaos. 76

The Terrible Two's, Aromatic Adventures. 78

Kids & Mayhem. 80

Firework Fiascos 84

Any Container Will Do, Product Switcheroos 85

Classroom Calamities. 87

Occupational Oopsies 87

Anger Management. 88

Pepper Spray, When Spice Meets Chaos 89

Random Calls. 90

Conclusion 95

National Helpline Phone Numbers 96

About the Author 98

"Should I induce vomiting, where can I get Ipecac?"

"Never induce vomiting unless instructed by the poison specialist."

Introduction

Sick Sad Stupid You Decide
Tales from the Poison Center

In these pages, you'll embark on a journey into a world most of us hope to avoid – the realm of poisoning emergencies. As you'll soon discover, this is not a book about despair; it's a testament to the extraordinary human capacity for resilience, learning, and hope.

The Poison Center is an unsung hero in our healthcare system, where dedicated professionals stand ready to answer desperate calls, offering guidance in moments of panic. These tales are not just stories; they're invaluable lessons, reminders that life can take unpredictable turns, and that knowledge and quick thinking can be the difference between life and death.

Prepare to be amazed, saddened, and sometimes, amused. In these real-life narratives, you'll find sickness, sadness, and stupidity, but you'll also find bravery, compassion, and wisdom.

Ultimately, "You Decide" is the heart of this book. It challenges you, the reader, to put yourself in the shoes of those who faced these crises. Learn from their experiences, and together, let's strive for a safer and wiser world.

Exploring the Path that Led Me to This Moment

In this book, I'll take you on a journey through my unexpected career in nursing, specifically in the challenging field of a poison specialist in a Poison Center. My path to this profession was far from conventional; it all started with a desire to earn quick money and avoid prolonged schooling. Back then, I was young and naïve. I believed that becoming a cosmetologist was the fastest route to financial stability. However, after getting my license and working for a few months my enthusiasm for this career waned, and I knew it wasn't the right fit for me.

Fortunately, I crossed paths with a young woman named Dot, while working at the salon. This encounter would change the course of my life. Dot was an incredible person who needed assistance due to a car accident when she was 18 years old. It left her paralyzed from the shoulders to her toes. She had a live-in caretaker, and I was fortunate enough to be able to help her part-time.

I had no idea that this experience with Dot would ultimately lead me to a career in nursing. Taking care of her not only allowed me to develop important caregiving skills but also drew on my background as a cosmetologist, which was a benefit Dot enjoyed.

After my time with Dot, I decided to pursue a career in nursing. I worked in Pediatrics while going to school. I initially thought I would continue working with children throughout my career. However, fate had other plans for me.

Upon completing my RN, I found myself working in an open-heart unit and later moving to a new city. It was there that I started working in a Level 1 Trauma Critical Care Unit. It turned out to be a perfect fit for my adrenaline-seeking nature. Eventually, I heard about an opportunity at my hospital's Poison Center and decided to make the transition. Little did I know that this move would define the rest of my nursing career.

In this book, I will share with you some captivating stories from my time in the Poison Center. While these tales are intriguing and may even "wow" you, my primary goal is to shed light on the critical importance of poison awareness and prevention. I want to emphasize how easily accidents can happen. It often takes just a moment of distraction—a phone call, visitors at home, or even a simple change in routine— to lead to a dangerous situation.

By sharing my experiences, I hope to raise awareness and help parents and caregivers understand that it can happen to anyone, and we all need to be vigilant in safeguarding against potential poisoning incidents. My hope is that these stories help prevent someone from injury.

Charisse A. Webb RN

Charisse Webb RN; CSPI

The History of Poison Centers, why do we need them?

In the early 1950s, the American Academy of Pediatrics recognized the need for specialized expertise in managing poison exposures. The first Poison Center was established in Chicago in 1953. Over the years, Poison Centers have evolved to provide 24/7 hotline services staffed by healthcare professionals.

Poison Centers are pivotal in assessing the effects of substances on human health. They provide immediate assistance, information, and data collection for poisonings, aiding emergency response, healthcare professionals, and public health efforts.

A Poison Specialist must access a wide range of resources to identify substances and products. They utilize toxicology databases, consult medical literature, government agencies, and manufacturer information, historical knowledge and collaboration with experts, in handling exposures to drugs, gases, plants, insects, snakes, chemicals, cleaning products, automotive items, toys, pesticides, cosmetics, personal care products, and commercial items—whether current or products that have been stored for 20-30 years.

The specialists at Poison Centers need to quickly find out what happened and assess the potential risks associated with (ingestion, eye contact, inhalation, or skin exposure).

> **The specialist needs to know what treatment is needed and they usually need to know right away!**

Poison Centers offer 24/7, cost-free expert advice over the phone, guiding and empowering callers to manage poisonings at home when it's safe. Their goal is not to discourage using emergency departments when necessary, but to help determine the best course of action, prioritizing safety. These centers have been considered one of the most successful and important public health programs in the United States.

National Poison Center
800-222-1222

To fulfill this role, Poison Centers are staffed with dedicated professionals, including nurses, pharmacists, and physicians, who are specially trained in clinical toxicology. The expertise of these staff members is of paramount importance. When individuals contact Poison Centers, they don't speak with operators but rather with highly trained and experienced experts who are available 24 hours a day.

Throughout the lifespan, Poison Centers help and promote poison prevention measures to ensure the safety of the public.

Home Hazards

A mother called 911 hysterically, stating "I'm dying, I'm dying." She said that her two-year-old threw the glass thermometer containing mercury on the ground, breaking the glass and mercury on the tile floor. The mother said there was a horrible odor. She was going to die from the vapors (usually no odor). EMS arrived on the scene to determine the odor was not related to mercury.

The odor was related to a skunk in the neighborhood, not mercury. The glass from the thermometer was easily cleaned up and chaos was averted. There is simple cleanup for this exposure.

What happens if I just dropped a mercury thermometer on the tile floor?

"The glass tube breaks, the mercury spills out on the tile floor."

Many people have a bottle of water sitting by their bedside. We commonly get a call from somebody taking a swallow of their 3% hydrogen peroxide or isopropyl alcohol, thinking it was their water bottle. Usually, it just takes one swallow for people to stop and realize they have made a terrible error. *I am unsure why there is a need for isopropyl alcohol or hydrogen peroxide at the bedside.*

—

A five-year-old found a beautiful locket at his grandparents' home while helping empty some boxes. It had a hinge, and he opened it up to find powder inside. The child thought it might be like a pixie stick. He thought the powder was candy. Upon sticking his finger in this powder, and tasting it, it was not as sweet tasting as he anticipated. He showed the locket to his mother who told him it was ashes inside. They were cremation ashes of a relative. Shortly thereafter, the child complained of a stomachache. *Children this age can be fatalistic. It was "Yucky" not poisonous.*

The Poison Center receives calls from someone hearing the carbon monoxide detector alarming; they want to know what to do. The problem remains if they stay where the alarm is going off. This is a gas that cannot be detected by smell, which is why we have monitors.

If your carbon monoxide detector alarm goes off, open your home and leave immediately.

A father in Florida called the Poison Control Center in a state of panic. His five-year-old child had come to him with a handful of mothballs. The child came to him stating "snowballs." Worried that the child may have ingested some of the mothballs, the father reached out for guidance.

There were no signs that the child had any of the mothballs in his teeth, nor did he have any of the odor on his breath. In a follow-up call, it was confirmed that the child had not developed any symptoms related to mothball ingestion.

—

During the pandemic, many households received multiple deliveries, often packed with small Styrofoam packing peanuts. These lightweight and easily chewable items can pique the curiosity of young children. While the risk of choking exists when children put such items in their mouths, the good news is that, if swallowed without choking, *Styrofoam packing peanuts are not poisonous.*

A caller asked, "I am on vacation, and I was trying to brush my teeth, but I accidentally grabbed my Benadryl cream instead of my toothpaste. Have I been poisoned?"

A mother called very upset that her 10-month-old had just eaten the dog poop that was on the floor. This was a healthy family pet. Although this would be disgusting, mom was relieved to know the poop wasn't poisonous.

Button batteries, commonly found in various household devices like remote controls, hearing aids, and more, can pose a serious risk when swallowed by anyone. In a specific case involving a 10-month-old, the child managed to open a remote control and swallowed one of these tiny button batteries. Unlike some larger objects, these batteries are easy to swallow, reducing the risk of choking.

However, the danger lies in their potential to become lodged in the esophagus. Once lodged, button batteries can cause severe burns and erosion of the esophageal tissue due to electrical and chemical reactions.

Therefore, it's crucial to take precautions by securing household items containing button batteries, keeping them out of reach of children. *If someone swallows a button battery call the Poison Center immediately. There are some steps you would be instructed do on the way to an emergency department.*

> One of the many household chemicals I was warned about when I started as a Poison Center nurse was hydrofluoric acid. It is used as a rust remover, but it's also used to etch glass—a horrible, deadly substance.

I've told all my friends and family about this scary chemical. I wanted to be sure everyone knew about it and the dangers involved.

Early in my poison career, I got a call from a flight crew who was at the scene of an outlying hospital where a young school-aged child had encountered hydrofluoric acid. The father was aware this was a 70% solution of this hydrofluoric acid, which even with a small amount of spill is potentially life-threatening. This child was playing in the yard when the bucket of acid was tipped over. She fell into the spill, accidentally sitting down into this chemical.

She got some on her bottom and it also dripped down her legs. This exposure happened at 4 o'clock in the afternoon. The initial emergency department decontaminated the child's skin by flushing with water. The first call I got regarding this incident was at 7 o'clock at night.

This child was in full cardiac arrest. Hydrofluoric acid can have direct effects on the heart, leading to irregular, and, sometimes, life-threatening heartbeats. The flight crew was given recommendations to help stabilize this young child. The flight crew was able to stabilize this girl to get her to a level one trauma center, where she went into cardiac arrest again.

By 10 o'clock that night, there was nothing more that could be done. This young child died in a very short time. This is one of those horrible chemicals I will never forget, and a death I also will never forget.

Superglue

Tales from the Sticky Side

Many of us may remember when Superglue first became popular. There was an ad where a gentleman applied glue to his hard hat and attached the hat to a board. Then, he placed the hat on his head and suspended his weight from the board. It was amazingly strong glue! One young man decided to test this. His girlfriend called us after he stuck his hand to his desk with superglue and could not get it off.

—

Another woman trying to be very clever, did not want to lose her beautiful earrings so she superglued them to her ears. She did not lose the earrings all evening. It is a good thing she loved these earrings; she wore them for a while!

—

A man who recently had eye surgery had been putting eye drops in one eye every two hours. He was tired. It was late. Reaching for the wrong container, he put one drop in his eye. It caused immediate burning. He quickly closed his eye; then he could not open it again. His wife discovered a superglue container by his eye drops. His eye was glued shut.

—

A 13-year-old, working on a science project at home, used superglue to glue marbles to a wire. His seven-year-old sibling entered the room, running over to grab some marbles.

The superglue stuck the marbles to his hand.

A World of Cleaning Products

The Soap Opera of Spills

The manager of the grocery store called us regarding a woman who had red and irritated hands after using chemicals on her hands. She touched a broken egg. Thinking it was poisonous, she went to the aisle with the cleaners and disinfectants. After spraying her hands with disinfectants, she required treatment for the irritation caused by the cleaning solutions.

—

It was cold and flu season. One mother decided to spray some disinfectants on the doorknobs at her home. Shortly thereafter, she found her two-year-old sucking on the doorknob. The child did not appear to be harmed by this.

—

A woman hopped out of the shower in a hurry to get to work. She did not put her glasses on and sprayed the bathroom cleanser detergent under her arm instead of deodorant.

—

A question came from a young lady, "Is porcelain paint poisonous?" The answer: it depends on what you did with the porcelain paint. This young lady confessed that she painted her teeth with it to whiten her teeth, and now was concerned that it was poisoning her because her gums were irritated and red.

> **Is porcelain paint poisonous?**
>
> **"It depends on what you did with the porcelain paint."**

During cold-flu and Covid season, there were a lot of disinfecting wipes around. Apparently, they were fun to play with. We had multiple toddlers who would pull out these little disinfecting wipes and stick them in their mouths. If they did not choke on them, they usually did well.

> **One of the hazards that you hear about quite frequently with children is that they can drown in a small amount of water.**

While a family was cleaning floors, there was a bucket containing a floor cleaner, bleach, and water. The bucket had about 4 inches of dirty water in it. The 10-month-old fell into the bucket, headfirst, nearly drowning.

The child required mechanical ventilator support for a long period of time due to the water and bacteria in his lungs. He also ended up with infections in both of his eyes from the dirty water getting into them.

> **The family turned away for a minute to tend to a sibling. Unfortunately, that's all it takes.**

One mother called from her car; she had just pulled over. Her 10-year-old was screaming in the background as she was trying to determine what had just happened to him. He was spitting. Finally, she found that he was eating brownies in the backseat of the car. The child stated, "he had nothing to drink so he sprayed a disinfectant cleaner in his mouth to try and swallow the brownie." The child was fine after some water. The mother was asked if the child was normally developed. She stated rather indignantly, "her child was fine!"

DIY Mishaps

How to turn Do it Yourself to DO NOT do it.

" *A clogged sink is a big problem that people like to handle by themselves, usually in the evening. The common approach is to pour all kinds of things into the drain.* "

When a gentleman poured a drain opener into the sink, it splashed back on the standing water, and it went into his open eyes.

Drain cleaners have a pH of about 13.5 and can cause severe damage to the skin, the eyes, and the lungs.

One fearless plumber wannabe decided he would pour some bleach down the sink drain. It didn't really help, so he poured a drain cleaner down that same drain. Immediately, chlorine gas formed.

The family had to evacuate the small house because the fumes were overwhelming. Then, they had to call for a plumber.

I bet it cost more money when your plumber must help you in a hazmat outfit.

24

There was a young man, very upset, calling to see if he got the wrong kind of superglue. He superglued part of his tooth that had broken off. Fortunately, or unfortunately, saliva will break down the superglue.

When the bond broke, he unfortunately swallowed the part of the tooth that was broken. *Now he was going to need real dental care, not DIY.*

—

The emergency department called regarding a 78-year-old woman who had nail polish that was thick and old, in the jar.

This patient decided she would put it in the microwave to loosen it up. After pulling it from the microwave, it exploded in her hand, sending shards of glass and silver nail polish up her hand, and into her arm. Silver pieces and glass had to be removed from the arm wounds.

"I was changing a light bulb and some rat feces dropped into my mouth. Am I going to die?"

Put this number in your phone, now!

**National Poison Center
800-222-1222**

Sex, Sex & More Sex

Quirky Sexcapades

A young man called very upset. He was experiencing redness pain he stated," the skin was sloughing off of his penis." He said he did not look at any of the products inside the shower before taking his glasses off. He apparently masturbated with a chemical hair removing product. These products are notorious for leaving chemical burns in sensitive areas.

—

This call was received at 6 AM after I had worked 11 hours already. A mother called stating this was the third time she caught her 14-year-old daughter having sex with the family dog. Unsure of where to go with this call, I asked where did she learn this behavior? The mother said, "here, you ask her" and put the daughter on the phone.

I asked this child where she learned this behavior. She declined to answer, but defiantly stated, "well, I can't get pregnant" and then disconnected the call. *I hope this family got some help. We handle a lot of calls. I am not sure why this mother believed the Poison Center was her best resource.*

—

During a disease outbreak, it was suggested that maybe we could inject bleach internally, but no one ever suggested bathing in bleach that I had heard of until...a gentleman called.

He was worried that he might have poisoned his girlfriend's unborn child. He informed me that he had bathed in bleach prior to having sex with his pregnant girlfriend. *I did not ask the reason for the bleach bath.*

It is very unusual for a 24-year-old that is otherwise healthy to need any help getting an erection. But a young 24-year-old decided he wanted to enhance the experience by having his young girlfriend inject an expanding foam through a straw into his penis.

This product is used to fill and seal gaps and expands and hardens quickly. The Poison Center was called by an emergency department to see if there was anything that would dissolve this foam without causing damage to the penis and urethra. *I suspect he was not able to have an erection for a while.*

—

Is it possible masturbating with WD-40 last night might have caused this?

A young man called early one morning to say he was having pain when he was urinating. The pain had just started this morning. Hesitantly, he asked, "Is it possible that masturbating with WD-40 last night might have caused this?"

A woman called, concerned that battery acid was leaking from her personal massager, panicking about acid burns in her "Twinkie." *Take note, one may want to inspect your personal massagers to determine that they are intact prior to use.*

—

A caller was concerned about the risk of infection due to his practice of coprophagia, which he explained involves eating feces for sexual gratification. *I learned many unusual things at work.*

> Consuming feces can expose one to a variety of harmful pathogens.
>
> This is not a healthy practice on many levels.

Wildlife

Reptile Wrangling, Tales of Scales

We all like to spend time outside enjoying the recreation of our choice in the fresh air. Being out in nature has many benefits: exercise, stress reduction, adventure, and just plain old fun.

However, it is good to know and understand the plants, animals, and insects that you may encounter that may cause you harm. Being able to identify them and avoid contact with them can save a lot of pain, suffering, and sometimes death.

The following are a few instances where the person did not use good judgment to avoid an unfortunate incident with a dangerous creature.

> Being able to identify harmful species and avoid contact can save a lot of pain, suffering, and sometimes death.

A 19-year-old man was out hiking when he came across a pygmy rattlesnake slithering across the trail in front of him. He thought it would be cool to take a selfie with this venomous creature to show his friends, so he picked it up, and of course, was promptly bitten on the finger. After this bite, he displayed some common sense and decided to contact the Poison Center. He was told to go to the emergency department for evaluation of this dangerous bite. The young man did as he was instructed.

After eight hours of observation in the emergency room at the local hospital, he showed no signs of swelling or coagulopathy. He was discharged, as the bite was determined to be a dry bite injecting no venom. The lucky young man went home with a story to tell, but no photo of him and the snake.

A father was riding his bike one day when he saw a snake crawling across the path he was riding on. The dad thought it would be a great surprise to bring the snake home to show his son who was fascinated by these reptiles. This snake was colorful, with red, yellow, and black bands around the snake. The dad got off his bike, grabbed up the snake and was immediately bitten on the finger. He had to pull the snake off that finger to grab it with the other hand, and he proceeded to ride along where he was bitten again on the other hand.

Being a good dad, he eventually arrived home with the snake only to be told by his eight-year-old son, who knew something about snakes that this was a coral snake, which had a very potent venom. The child recognized the pattern of banded stripes on the snake. He remembered "Red stripes on yellow stripes kills a fellow."

The dad called 911 and was referred to the poison hotline he was given some instructions: No cutting. No sucking. No tourniquet. No medicine. He was then referred to the nearest emergency department for treatment. After getting the 911 call, the poison specialist located the antidote and assisted with treatment.

> Coral snakes have alternating red, black and yellow bands that circle the body of the snake. They can be confused with the King Snake, a non-venomous snake that has the same colored bands. To identify a Coral Snake: "Red on yellow, kills a fellow. Red on black, venom lack."

> Eastern Diamondback Rattlesnakes are venomous reptiles, and their bites can be life-threatening, particularly for young children.

In a tragic incident, a 911 dispatcher contacted a Poison Center when a young toddler was bitten by an Eastern Diamondback Rattlesnake on the leg. Despite immediate medical attention and transportation to a children's hospital emergency room, the child tragically did not survive the snakebite.

Despite the best efforts of medical professionals, the severity of the bite and the rapid onset of symptoms contributed to the unfortunate outcome in this case.

This serves as a reminder of the importance of snakebite awareness and the need for swift and expert medical intervention when snakebites occur, especially with venomous species like the Eastern Diamondback Rattlesnake.

> **In the Poison Center we have the "7T's," most common characteristics of a snakebite victim: Testosterone · Teenager Tequila · Teasing · Toothless Driving Trucks · Tattoos.**

There was a young man who had a party involving alcohol. He brought out his pet copperhead snake. The man put it around his neck to show his friends. He was promptly bitten on the neck, where he developed significant swelling, which sent him to the emergency room.

—

An 82-year-old man was resting in his recliner in his backyard when a frog jumped on his face and secreted in his eyes, causing a great deal of irritation. The man was able to remove his contact lenses, and then flush with some contact lens solution, but he continued to have irritation. He put some Visine in his eyes to help relieve the irritation. The eye was still irritated an hour later.

> **Water is the best eye flush when you are at home.**

Insects & Creepy Crawlers

Bloopers of Bug Encounters

A man in a rural county said he was bitten by an unknown insect a few days earlier. He stated, "The bite left a crater in my belly, so I put Ipecac (an oral medication used to induce vomiting) into the crater to force the poison out. Now, that crater has thick smelly drainage in it, and it hurts."

—

> A young man called to report, "A spider bit me." Do you know what kind of spider? "Yep. I got it right here... pause... Dang, it bit me again!"

A 46-year-old woman came into the emergency department very upset that there were worms crawling around in her ears, her nose, and her throat—although she had never seen the worms. She had been attempting to get rid of them. To treat herself, three days earlier, she took a liquid puppy worming medication (250 mg of piperazine) which made her vomit. Then, she drank castor oil and garlic, which she believed made the worms mad. She is now asking what else she can do to treat this.

—

Touching some caterpillars can be quite painful. Their little hairs can get embedded under the skin and can cause a lot of pain if you don't get them out. A caller stated that he picked up a furry caterpillar and now is having pain going from his fingers to his "limpnoids" (AKA -lymph nodes/arm pit).

Marine Life

Fishy Fiascos

Knowledge is power. One thing that you learn when you live close to the coast is there are stingrays out there and you need to learn the "stingray shuffle." If you do not, those stingrays like to flip their barbed tails up if you accidentally step on them. The barbs are most likely to hit your feet and lower legs. I understand it's quite painful. "Stingray shuffle" warns the rays you are coming, so they move out of the way.

There are other creatures to be aware of when you are wandering along in the water, like jellyfish. They have bodies that look like a gelatinous bag with tentacles that can sting. They are beautiful animals, but if they touch you or accidentally touch them it can be painful.

—

One man called reporting that his friend was stung by some jellyfish. He knew that if he urinated on the area that was stung, it would stop the stinging. His friend was not going to let that happen.

As much as you need to learn the plants and animals that surround you in your yard, and in your parks, those of us that live on the water must be aware of what's in the water. I used to be afraid to go in the water. Now, I can treat almost everything that happens.

" Note to self; when you're at the beach if you don't want your friend to pee on you, bring vinegar to stop the stingers from firing. "

Pesticides

Pest Control Misadventures

A young man was trying to open a bottle of pesticide and broke the glass bottle. It spilled into the open cut on his hand. He put a rag on his hand and held pressure on it to stop the bleeding, but it continued to have a lot of pain. So, he took the bandage off and squeezed the cut on his hand to get it to bleed to get the poison out. He then flushed it with some water.

His friend thought it was a good idea to get an industrial strength cleaner and they used that to clean the wound on his hand. The pain got even more intense, so he poured whiskey on it. When he called the Poison Center, he was asked to flush it with water—and then the call dropped.... *A few minutes later, his friend called back to say that his friend was not looking very good. He had put a tourniquet on his arm to keep the poison from going into his body.*

—

"Was this related to the lice cream?"

One young man had been putting a lice treatment on his skin for scabies for the previous few days. He called the Poison Center, very upset, saying, "The bed is moving, and my friend looks like a cheesecake, I want to eat him. Was this related to the lice cream?"

—

The little blue rat pellets that are used to kill mice and rats are enticing to children. They are beautifully colored and usually blue. They are small and they are easy to put in the mouth. There are frequent calls regarding young toddlers, who manage to get the little blue rat pellets in their mouth, mistaking them for candy.

Plant Perils

There are some plants that are problems for gardeners. Frequently, people tend to trim their pencil cactus, and, if you don't have gloves on or don't have eye protection, that sap gets into your eyes, or from your hands into your eyes. It can be very irritating.

On occasion, people are proactive and want to know if their gift is going to poison someone. A mother wanted to give a hydrangea plant, on the first day of school, to the teacher. She wanted to know if the plant was poisonous. What a great thing to think about plants! *Generally, this plant is not poisonous if nobody eats it.*

A mother called with a child screaming in the background. The mother stated that the two-year-old bit into a philodendron plant. After getting something to drink, the child was fine.

A proactive dad was about to go on vacation with his three-year-old child. He called to ask, "I want to know if it's OK to use DEET insect repellent on my child."

"This is a pesticide that can be dangerous depending on the concentration of the Deet. Good question, Dad!"

Baby Intoxication

A mother with two of her daughters was at the hair salon to get beautiful for a wedding. One of the daughters had her two-month-old baby with her while they were getting ready. She was feeding the baby. She pulled some water from the refrigerator at the nail salon and mixed it with the baby formula. Unfortunately, there was vodka in the water bottle. The child became unresponsive and required medical care.

—

A six-month-old child was brought into the emergency department. She was very lethargic. Apparently, her formula was mixed with vodka (just like the previous example). It was supposed to be water in the refrigerator. The baby's initial blood alcohol level was very high after three hours in the emergency department; it continued to rise for a few hours. The family said that apparently, the baby was reluctant to drink this. *Small wonder, this child knew this was not right!*

Young parents that are feeding formula to babies are tired. They probably haven't slept much.

A father called one evening. His seven-month-old baby was vomiting. He mixed the baby formula accidentally with some laundry detergent instead of plain water.

Babies naturally have a unique "new baby smell," but some families choose to add perfume to their infants. A child's thought if it smells pleasant, it must taste good. However, perfume contains alcohol, which can lower blood sugar levels in children. The silver lining is that sugar serves as an antidote, and children enjoy sweet treats. *If you can provide them with something sweet to drink, it may help counteract the effects of low blood sugar.*

—

With the increasing popularity of vape devices, it has become quite easy for young children to access either nicotine or THC. Even a small amount of nicotine can pose a serious poisoning risk for youngsters, as it can lead to seizures and is easily absorbed through the skin or by ingesting. *It's essential to exercise caution and ensure that vaping devices and cartridges are kept out of reach of children.*

—

A creative six-year-old was playing outside with his parents while they were painting the house with green latex paint. In a spontaneous decision, the young child thought it would be a good idea to paint his two-year-old brother green as well. Mom became concerned, worrying that the paint might be absorbed through the skin. *This incident presented one of those memorable photo opportunities. A quick wash with soap and water would effectively remove the paint, ensuring that all would be no longer green. Next time purple?*

—

A mother residing in a homeless shelter had placed a laundry pod on top of the basket while preparing to do her laundry. The basket was on the bed, with her 15-month-old child. Unfortunately, the child managed to pop the laundry pod in her mouth. The laundry pod burst, which is highly dangerous due to the concentrated contents

—

An 18-month-old child wandered into the bathroom, discovering toothpaste and proceeded to eat it. Toothpaste typically contains fluoride, which can be quite irritating to the stomach. To alleviate any discomfort, it's advisable to provide the child with a small amount of milk or calcium-fortified orange juice. The calcium can help counter the effects of fluoride ingestion.

Suicide

> *Sometimes you wonder what was happening in somebody's mind to do some of the things that we are told about.*

A 62-year-old woman was found unconscious in a wedding dress. She had crushed up an unknown amount of medication into a paste and swallowed it. The paste was still around her face and caked inside her mouth. The medications she had available were Prozac, and Trazodone.

—

It is unfathomable how a parent feels when they find their child who has tried to commit suicide. EMS called the Poison Center in reference to a mother who found her 19-year-old child cyanotic, hanging from a homemade noose. She also found that she had 90 Prozac pills missing from a new prescription bottle. The young man was able to be resuscitated.

—

An emergency room had called the Poison Center. They had an adult man who was brought into the emergency department to sober up. He had had too much alcohol. The main reason the Poison Center was called, when he had sobered up and they were discharging him, he was not ready to go home yet. So, he had a bottle of baclofen in his bag. He opened and tipped the bottle into his mouth, swallowing the pills. This kept him in the hospital a few days longer for treatment and evaluation.

There are no great ways to commit suicide, but there was a patient who poured muriatic acid down his throat to try and kill himself. That is a horrible way to die. This person did not die but will likely require multiple surgeries and tube feedings for a long period of time due to the damage caused by the acid.

—

A 68-year-old man came into the emergency room very depressed; he notified the staff that he had eaten rat bait two hours prior to arrival. He was treated and his blood work was monitored over a few days. They then discharged him. Despite the medical attention and care he received; the man's psychological struggles persisted. The next day the same man came to another emergency room after eating more rat bait. The Poison Center was called about the previous exposure, and we were called on the second one as well.

The emergency department staff was notified this man was just recently discharged from another hospital. He was again treated then monitored for a few days. Later that same day, six hours after his discharge, this man went to a third emergency department. It became apparent that the man was in dire need of psychiatric intervention. After this visit, medically cleared, they transferred him to a psychiatric facility.

> The story is, indeed, a reminder of the complexity of mental health issues. Individuals, in deep distress, may turn to hospitals for comfort and help, even if their actions are ultimately harmful to themselves.

It is unknown why an 85-year-old gentleman took an overdose of Tylenol p.m. and his primidone the night before this call. His wife called 911 at 9:30 AM to say her husband took drugs last night, fell and never got up. She told EMS the fall was at 10 o'clock PM, the night before. He was still on the floor when EMS arrived, minimally responsive. She waited until the next day since he was still alive and decided to call 911, and told the EMS responders, "Get him out of here."

—

Unfortunately, for some people, the emergency department is their safe place. A 60-year-old man with HIV came to the emergency department with chest pain. He was worked up and discharged to home. He became very angry and not ready to go home, so he found a bottle of his Ativan, 2 mg pills, and swallowed a bunch of them to harm himself. This kept him in the hospital several hours longer.

—

A patient with increased paranoia due to PTSD had difficulty handling his emotional problems. The 41-year-old was brought into the emergency department by his parents, increasingly paranoid. He did not recognize his parents and talked about killing them. He would not get out of the car outside of the emergency department because he was afraid of an explosion. He told the emergency department, if the building could not withstand a blast, he would not go in.

Reassured, he entered the hospital and let the staff know that he had taken an unknown amount of Lunesta pills to treat the voices in his head.

A few days after Christmas a 41-year-old mother called the Poison Center. She reported having just taken a large overdose of her medicines. When asked why she did this, she responded "My children made me sad at Christmas."

—

To get out of jail, some of prisoners would prefer to spend time in the emergency department. One such emergency department called after an inmate from the local correctional institution came to the hospital. He had eaten several objects: three toenail clippers, two AA batteries, and three magnesium pills, as well as ten unknown blood thinner pills and two of his own Seroquel pills. He remained alert. According to the x-ray of his abdomen, multiple objects were identified...

—

One patient showed up in the emergency room confused; he was only able to tell us he had taken $7 worth of Benadryl and was not sure how many pills were available. . ??????????????

> Sometimes it's difficult for a poison specialist to get the information needed, either by EMS or a hospital, about what patients might have taken.
>
> Some patients are very vague about what they're going to tell concerning what they did or took. When a patient says they have taken pills in the hospital, it is so much easier to treat them if we know what drugs where available to them and how much they took.

The maid dialed 911 upon discovering a man who had ingested antifreeze and whiskey, displaying symptoms of poisoning. He left a suicide note. Antifreeze can inflict severe brain and kidney harm, but the whiskey likely spared his kidneys. Ethanol in whiskey impedes the conversion of antifreeze chemicals into toxic substances, safeguarding his kidneys from damage. However, he still had a long road to recovery.

—

A woman called crying, very upset. She was having severe belly pain and vomiting. She said, "I am done." She took 50 Ibuprofen to end it all. Not wanting an ambulance, she wanted to know what symptoms she would experience before she died. She wanted me to stay on the phone so she would not die alone. *This is not the first time someone wanted me to stay on the phone while they died, refusing medical help.* She did get some help when the pain increased.

—

The 16-year-old wanted to avoid returning to school after spring break. Her solution was to take a large dose of painkillers when her mother left the house. She then wrote a long suicide note on her arm, from her shoulder to her fingers.

—

A 58-year-old man presented to the emergency room having ingested 39 tablets of Diltiazem, each 180 mg, a few hours prior. His dangerously low blood pressure indicated a severe overdose, potentially leading to life-threatening cardiovascular complications. He was able to get good supportive medical intervention necessary to stabilize him.

An emergency department called regarding a 35-year-old man who had taken 30 Abilify and 30 Lorazepam pills, according to his wife. Those were the pills she knew were missing. She also suspected that he might have taken some of her Lyrica and Amitriptyline pills.

> In situations like this, having family or friends who can provide vital information is invaluable. Their insights can expedite medical evaluation and treatment decisions, ensuring a more accurate diagnosis and appropriate care.
>
> With the wife's crucial information, healthcare providers could quickly assess the potential risks and interactions of the medications involved. This man received the help he needed.

A man, in his late 70s, well-versed in chemicals and pesticides, ingested organophosphate pesticide while his wife and daughter were out. Upon their return, they found him experiencing severe symptoms such as vomiting, diarrhea, and diminished consciousness.

Tragically, he passed away shortly after being taken to the hospital. It was later revealed that he had left a suicide note indicating he was suffering from metastatic cancer.

A 50-year-old patient with a history of seizures ingested an unspecified quantity of Tramadol and Valproic acid the previous night, possibly experiencing a seizure. When EMS arrived at their home, the family reported that he just did this four days also. He just got out of the hospital the day before and did it again.

Suicide Pacts, Desperate Decisions

An 81-year-old man had a suicide pact with his wife. They both took large amounts of pills to kill themselves. He stated, she was not dying quick enough, so he put a pillow over her head and started stabbing her with a knife. Both patients were in critical condition. They survived the overdose from pills. The wife needed more treatment for her stab wounds.

—

The emergency department called the Poison Center. Twin 20-year-old girls were found at home. One young lady was dead at the scene. The other one died the next day. They both had apparently taken an overdose of pills with the intention of killing themselves.

—

Two 13-year-old twin sisters in a suicide pact both ate Acetaminophen 500 mg pills days prior to presenting at the hospital with severe abdominal pain and vomiting. Both young ladies were in liver failure and required treatment.

Culinary Capers

Confessions of a Confused Cook

A woman called very upset. She said that her husband had cooked chicken for them for dinner and it tasted terrible. She went into the kitchen to see what he had used. Instead of cooking oil, he used lemon oil furniture polish to cook the chicken in by mistake. Neither of them had any symptoms—just a bad taste in their mouths.

> **Thanksgiving can be a confusing time for a lot of cooks in the kitchen.**

A family called on Thanksgiving Day. They had been remodeling their kitchen. They made some gravy with what they thought was flour to thicken the gravy. Apparently, it was a little Plaster of Paris. It did not harden in the gravy, and her guests ate it. The host of this event wanted to know, "Do I have to tell the people that I invited what happened?"

—

This family put the turkey in the oven and set it for 250° for 12 hours. One sister thought the other sister had turned the oven on. It turned out no one turned the oven on, so the turkey sat in the oven all night and now they want to know, "Can we cook it and eat it today?"

A wife called because her husband was cooking the turkey. He had been basting it over a couple of hours when she checked on it. She thought it had an unusual smell to it, so she asked him what he was basting it with? He pointed to a container that she earlier had put had bleach water in.

—

> **When in doubt throw it out!**

The family had decided to put their Thanksgiving turkey into a cooking bag. When they went to check on it the bag had ripped so they put the turkey and the bag into a large garbage bag and continued to cook it. The plastic garbage bag melted all over the turkey. They were wondering if they could still eat it.

The call was disconnected before I could respond.

About an hour later the same caller with the turkey in the bag said, "Thanks for the help, but we contacted our Puerto Rican cable guy who told us it should be fine to eat."

—

A woman from Florida called on a summer day, asking if she could eat the pork that she had left out in her car all night the night before. My inside voice said, "If you like having vomiting and diarrhea."

> **My inside voice said, "If you like having vomiting and diarrhea."**

Season's Eatings

and Festive Follies

One woman was started on a new medicine. Her husband stated, she had been under a lot of stress lately. The new medication was an anti-anxiety drug called Clonazepam. She had taken two pills before she went to bed. Her husband heard her up about an hour later and thought she might have taken another pill. He woke up to her baking the Christmas cards and wanted to know if she had overdosed on her medications.

—

A woman coming home from a three-day vacation found her refrigerator power had gone off. Most of the food was thawed but still cold. She wanted to know if she could refreeze this food and eat it later.

—

The day after Thanksgiving is the best time to get all the Thanksgiving bargains. One thrifty woman, early the day after Thanksgiving, took one of her husband's stimulant drugs and a half of pot of coffee and decided to go Christmas shopping. She ended up very dehydrated with chest pains in the mall.

> He woke up to her baking the Christmas cards and wanted to know if she had overdosed on her medications.

Beauty Blunders

A young woman was getting filmed by her boyfriend and wanted some very good, clean butt shots. However, she had some blemishes that she decided needed to be removed, so she decided to use a drain cleaner on her skin to remove those blemishes. *The drain cleaner caused redness, pain, and blistering. This is not going to be a pretty picture for a while.*

—

A woman called. She went to a person she met on the Internet to get a butt lift. The person doing the butt lift was using a product designed to be injected into an automobile tire. She allowed this person to inject it into her buttocks. She called because she had an infection and drainage coming from the area that she had been injected into.

—

The mother was dying her hair. She put all the hair dye on her hair but had a little bit left in a bowl. It was time to rinse out her hair. While she rinsed her hair, her three-year-old decided to eat what was left in the bowl of hair color.

—

Another mother, using a chemical hair straightener, had some left over on a stick. Mom put the stick in the garbage. Her 3-year-old, who was playing in the garbage, found the stick and put it in her mouth. That caused swelling in and around her mouth.

Glamour Mayhem

Children watch their parents put on cologne and make-up. In their little brains, if it's a good idea for their parents, it is a good idea for them.

> After reassuring parents the child will be fine, I have been known to pleasantly suggest that someone take a photo to remember this event!

Why not try some?

A young mother called because she found her three-year-old with a mouth full of body lotion. When asked how much she thought the child might have gotten, she said disgustedly—too much! The child vomited twice. That was the extent of the lotion on the child.

—

A mother called regarding her youngster who had red lipstick all over her mouth, and teeth. She had eaten some of it. *These are the kinds of calls that are not poisonous.*

Home Remedies

The Cure is Sometimes Worse Than the Poison: When Healing Hurts

A 16-year-old took many antidepressants to kill herself. When the mother found her, to save her, the mother gave the daughter a stick of butter to eat. Then, she put an emery board down her throat to induce vomiting. The young lady vomited several times and became dizzy. *Butter, and/or an emery board, should never be part of the cure.*

Call the Poison Center FIRST!

National Poison Center 800-222-1222

Is this number in your phone yet?

The mother of a five-year-old found her child with his face and body all red. He was crying. The family found that five Niacin pills (500 mg each) were missing. They put the child in an ice bath. When he became bluish, he was brought to the emergency department. They were not able to register a rectal temperature on this child; he was so cold. *This treatment would NEVER be recommended. Call the Poison Center, "first do no harm." Niacin flush can happen.*

A man was having dental problems. He had a toothache that had been going on for several days, so he took Tylenol 500 mg. He took three or four pills every couple of hours for a couple of days. Unfortunately, that amount of Tylenol in that short a period can cause liver damage.

This man's family called the Poison Center after he developed severe abdominal pain and vomiting. When he presented to the emergency department, he was in liver failure.

A 20-year-old nursing student was trying to study for her state boards. She started by drinking espresso which had quite a bit of caffeine. Still having trouble studying, she took some Methylphenidate pills, which is a stimulant medication that she borrowed from a friend with ADHD. She decided since it was getting to be early morning, she would drink a few Red Bull drinks.

Her roommate called saying that she was nauseated, vomiting, and that her heart rate was very high. She was also having chest pain. Sometimes sleep is the best answer, not drugs or chemicals.

> *Sometimes sleep is the best answer, not drugs or chemicals.*

—

A young girl took two ibuprofens for a headache. After showing her mother the bottle of ibuprofen, her mother noticed that the drug had expired five years ago. The mother told her to drink some olive oil and induce vomiting. The young lady was unable to vomit. The family called the Poison Center. It was determined no treatment was necessary. *Olive oil is not usually recommended as an antidote for poisons.*

—

A young man arrived in the emergency department with a cough, and a temperature of 102F. He answered to his name but fell asleep when not coughing. Apparently, his friends tried to treat his symptoms with gasoline. They gave him gasoline to drink and poured the gas all over his body. It was determined he had the flu and pneumonia. He was admitted and treated for the gasoline exposure and pneumonia.

Natural Disasters

> A hurricane is the perfect storm—providing too many unfortunate opportunities for poisonous situations to occur.

Hurricanes cause their own set of problems. At the onset of a hurricane, people board up their windows and attempt to evacuate.

Hurricanes force snakes and spiders to leave their homes as well, elevating the risk for poisonous bites and stings.

During a hurricane, families are all sheltering in place with children and elderly parents and grandparents. Adding family and friends brings potentially life-threatening medical conditions and medication to go along with them.

When you pull these people together, families get stressed, because they are out of their routines. Children get into medicines and cleaning products. The elderly can get confused about how much medicine they're taking; they sometimes take too much, or they take somebody else's.

When the power goes out, food poisoning begins. People don't want to throw away their food. Having no refrigeration, they try to eat it.

People needing to regain power, temporarily running their generators inside, where they can get carbon monoxide poisoning. If they siphon gasoline from their cars and lawnmowers to fuel their generators, it can accidentally be aspirated into their lungs.

It was a hurricane coming into the Gulf of Mexico. A woman called from the coastal community asking if someone could come to her home. During this tropical storm, it rained for several days.

She had water in her house and maggots were coming out of her carpet.

Can someone get rid of them?

Matters of Faith

Divine Dilemmas

There were religious rituals that I knew nothing about. I didn't realize that I would learn about them while in the Poison Center.

There are such things as purification rituals that go on for a few days. These include water, saunas, and vitamins, such as niacin, thiamine, as well as some others.

There was a young lady who became confused, disoriented, hallucinating, and persistently vomiting. She was brought into the emergency room after one such multi-day purification ritual. She was quite dehydrated—and needed treatment for a few days.

Punishment vs Abuse

These are always difficult situations where child services need to intervene in sometimes horrible situations:

The Poison Center was called regarding a three-year-old, whose family said had fallen while playing. This child came with a high heart rate and pinpoint pupils. For some unknown reason, the child had alcohol and opiates in her system and significant damage to her liver. She also had an open wound to the side of her head.

There was a suspicious story regarding her fall, and no explanation for the alcohol or drugs. This child's home life was evaluated by child services. *There is NO reason a toddler should have alcohol in their blood.*

A female called Poison Center from another state, stating that an assailant was pouring dishwashing detergent from the bottle into a seven-year-old's mouth. The child could be heard coughing and choking in the background. The female stated that the police were on their way.

The Poison Center that would have gotten a hospital call regarding this child was contacted to follow up to be sure the child received care. We were told the child was being evaluated.

The assailant, in this case, was the stepfather. He told the police that this child was disrespectful and was being punished.

Pets

Saliva Showdown of Germs

A frantic woman called while driving with her friend and a dog in the passenger seat. The dog had encountered a Bufo toad and stopped breathing. She was performing mouth-to-snout resuscitation but reported numbness in her mouth, likely from the toad's toxin.

I advised that Bufo toad toxins can induce respiratory paralysis in animals. I recommended continuing to the vet but suggested calling 911 if the woman's symptoms got worse.

—

The father called about his son's pet chicken, which was attacked by a fox and subsequently died despite mouth-to-beak resuscitation efforts. His concern was whether they could get rabies if the fox had it and passed it to the chicken. The risk of rabies transmission from a fox to humans through a chicken in this scenario is exceedingly low.

> "The risk of rabies transmission from a fox to humans through a chicken in this scenario is exceedingly low."

—

A woman called seeking guidance on how to handle her deceased cat, which had been under her bed for two weeks. She was looking for advice on the appropriate steps to clean up and potentially bury the cat.

My ferret ingested my birth control pills and part of the container. He seems fine currently. Will he be okay? Additionally, what steps should I take regarding birth control since it's no longer available?

> **Taste of gasoline is not poisonous, taste of dog tongue… not recommended.**

A woman was distressed, having put her tongue in her dog's mouth, and suspected the dog had licked spilled gasoline. She also experienced a similar gasoline taste in her mouth.

A concerned mother called regarding her one-year-old child who had ingested the pet cat's vomit. While certainly unpleasant, this act is not typically considered poisonous. Cat vomit, though unappealing, usually contains nothing toxic that would pose a serious health risk to a child. In most cases, the child should be fine.

A woman concealed her dog's medication for itching inside a piece of hotdog, but the family dog rejected it, spitting it out. However, a 10-month-old child unintentionally consumed the hotdog with the medication. This type of medication was not poisonous for the child.

The caller was distressed, suspecting his dog had been intentionally poisoned by a neighbor due to the dog's sickness, and refusal to eat, or drink. He sought information about potential poisons for dogs.

Various substances can be toxic to dogs, including certain foods like chocolate and grapes, household chemicals, plants, and medications. .

> It's essential to consult a veterinarian immediately if poisoning is suspected to diagnose and treat the specific toxin involved.

"My neighbor does not like my dog and poisoned him.

Where can I get the dog and the food tested for poisons?"

Sharing Animal Medication

A pig farmer called in after accidentally poking himself in the leg with a contaminated needle while vaccinating one of his pigs. As a precautionary measure, he would need to update his tetanus vaccine.

Pets With a Bite

A teenager, working at a pet store, was assigned to clean the lionfish tank without being informed of the potential danger posed by lionfish. During the cleaning process, the teenager was stung by a lionfish, resulting in considerable pain, swelling, and redness.

Lionfish are known for their venomous spines and are considered invasive species. The sting can cause painful symptoms and even complications if not treated. In such cases, obtain first aid information from the Poison Center when it's advisable to seek medical attention to address the effects of the venom and receive appropriate care for the wound.

Talk to an expert

**ASPCA Animal Poison Center
888-426-4435**

(this is not a free service)

Drug Abuse

Mischief in the World of Drug Testing

The young man was facing a federal job application that required a drug screening and expressed a lack of clean friends to provide urine. He asked if using a monkey or dog's urine would be a viable alternative. He stated, "I have no clean friends."

—

A woman called, extremely upset. She recently learned that she was pregnant, which was a good thing! However, she reported having been smoking marijuana for several weeks and was looking for detox options.

> He asked if using a monkey or dog's urine would be a viable alternative.

—

Another young man in his 20s called complaining that his throat was so sore he could not swallow his Oxycodone, so he crushed it and smoked it last night. His question, "Am I going to die?" My inside voice said, not today but very soon if you keep this up.

—

An 18-year-old called in a state of extreme confusion, claiming to be a duck, and expressing concern about saving imaginary ducklings. He explained that he and his father had taken LSD, leading to the hallucinations of being ducks. Despite advising him to call 911 for assistance, he insisted he couldn't because he believed he had wings.

Happy Hour on the Orthopedic Unit

A patient that had recently had her hip surgery asked for some tomato juice. A short time later checking on her, she was found unresponsive—after mixing her hand sanitizer with the tomato juice to make herself a very stiff, bloody Mary.

—

A 38-year-old individual, despite feeling tired, decided to proceed with his gym workout. He took a stimulant drug before exercising. Approximately 30 minutes into his workout, he became unresponsive and required CPR due to a heart attack. Fortunately, he recovered from this cardiac event.

> This incident serves as a stark reminder of the potential risks associated with the use of stimulant drugs, particularly in conjunction with exercise.

—

A woman with a cold experienced dizziness and blurred vision after doubling her dose of cough medicine containing Dextromethorphan to expedite its effectiveness. More is not always better.

" **More is not always better.** "

A man in his 40s arrived at the emergency department with severe skin issues; one of his arms exhibited sloughing skin, revealing exposed beefy red tissue. This condition was likely a result of exposure to contaminated cocaine, possibly containing Levamisole, a substance often found in adulterated drugs.

The severe skin reaction resembled Stevens-Johnson syndrome, a rare but severe disorder. His condition deteriorated to the extent that he required the amputation of one hand because of the complications stemming from the contaminated drug exposure.

—

A 75-year-old individual dialed 911 to report that someone had laced his crack cocaine with rat bait, and he had smoked it. He was having chest pain, shortness of breath, chills, and vomiting. This situation is a medical emergency, as rat poison can cause serious health issues.

—

The Poison Center received an uncommon call from a newborn nursery. A mother, worried about receiving inadequate pain medication during childbirth, resorted to drinking vodka when she began experiencing contractions. She arrived at the labor and delivery unit in a lethargic state with slurred speech.

Six hours after giving birth, alcohol was still detected in the baby's bloodstream.

> No baby should ever have alcohol in their bloodstream, as it poses severe risks to the infant's health and development.

In a harrowing incident driven by desperation related to drug use, a young couple both sought to use methamphetamines, with the young woman consuming it first. This led to a heated altercation, and tragically, the boyfriend slit the throat of his girlfriend to retrieve the meth.

Unfortunately, the woman lost her life because of this desperate and horrific event, underscoring the devastating consequences that substance abuse and addiction can have on individuals and their relationships.

> The opioid epidemic affects hospitals, emergency rooms, and families daily. The widespread availability of Narcan, an opioid reversal medication, is essential.
>
> It should be accessible to everyone because the need for it is present everywhere, given the pervasive nature of the opioid crisis.

In the hospital emergency room, patients occasionally present with extremely high temperatures, such as 107°F. Prolonged exposure to such elevated temperatures is detrimental to both the brain and major organs.

A 39-year-old patient with a history of ecstasy and crack cocaine abuse arrived with a high temperature, elevated heart rate, and blood pressure. Although he survived the episode, unfortunately, his kidneys did not, emphasizing the severe toll that extreme hyperthermia and substance abuse can take on the body's vital organs.

> This incident highlights the importance of recognizing and responding promptly to signs of a potential overdose.

A woman in her mid 50s was observed falling out of her car at a park at a children's soccer game. She was able to get back in the car where she remained motionless inside the vehicle for approximately two hours, raising concerns among bystanders. Eventually, one of the witnesses called for emergency medical services (EMS).

Upon examination, it was discovered that she had ingested a significant overdose of anti-anxiety and anti-depressant medications, which likely contributed to her incapacitated state.

> "If you see something, say something. This is someone's daughter, mother, sister..."

This incident highlights the importance of recognizing and responding promptly to signs of a potential overdose. If you see something say something. This is someone's daughter, mother, sister...

—

A 29-year-old male chewed and swallowed a fentanyl patch to get high and was discovered unresponsive by his mother. She had Narcan on hand and administered it to revive him. Many families find themselves in similar situations, where the need to use Narcan is both comforting and scary.

Running from the Police

Emergency calls often involve fugitives attempting to evade the police by ingesting drugs. In these situations, some individuals swallow handfuls, or entire bags, of pills.

Unfortunately, complications can arise, such as in the case of a gentleman who became unresponsive and stopped breathing after swallowing a baggie of pills. *These actions can have life-threatening consequences due to drug toxicity when the baggie opens or choking hazards.*

Mushrooms

Three teenagers ingested mushrooms that they picked in a field. One of them developed severe liver damage, requiring a potential liver transplant. Although the other two did experience liver problems, they were lucky and recovered. Picking wild mushrooms without expertise, especially without proper identification, can have severe and even life-threatening consequences. Unless you're a mycologist with in-depth knowledge of fungi, it's strongly advised to avoid randomly foraging for mushrooms to prevent potential harm or poisoning.

—

A man called to say that he ate an Amanita mushroom 2 to 3 years ago. He never had any symptoms but wanted to know what the long-term effects were. He was playing a video game and a mushroom popped up in the monitor, so, he called the Poison Centers thinking he was having a "flash back."

—

A man called stating he had a mushroom growing from his bunion because he had mold in his house.

Forms of Alcohol

A child's exploration with aftershave led to a potentially dangerous situation. Aftershave often contains ethanol, which can be absorbed through the skin. In this case, the child not only applied it to their body but also ingested some by drinking it.

Most children will not take more than a swallow. This smells nice but would not taste very good. However, this child was developmentally delayed and ingested a few ounces of the after shave.

Ethanol can lower blood sugar levels, leading to symptoms such as lethargy and could potentially be life-threatening. When a child ingests a substance like ethanol that can lead to decreased blood sugar levels, providing glucose is a common treatment. Glucose helps to counteract the effects of the ethanol by increasing the blood sugar levels.

> **Most frequent callers to the Poison Center are caregivers of young children.**

A man was found unresponsive with a large bottle of mouthwash. Drinking mouthwash, is a behavior often associated with individuals struggling with alcohol addiction. The high alcohol content in some mouthwashes makes them a potential target for those seeking alcohol when other sources aren't available or accessible.

Unfortunately, while mouthwash might contain a significant amount of alcohol, it's not meant for consumption. The presence of someone consuming mouthwash is a sign that they might be in a desperate situation, seeking any available alcohol, and likely in need of professional help and support for alcohol addiction.

Addiction

While we have systems in place for incarcerating drug offenders, we often fall short when it comes to effective treatment and prevention. Uninsured individuals can face even greater challenges accessing timely drug treatment.

When they reach out, they urgently need care, but it can be difficult to secure a spot in a treatment program on the same day, despite experiencing significant withdrawal symptoms, anxiety, vomiting, shakiness, and strong cravings for the substance they're trying to quit.

—

Joe, a 48-year-old cab driver, whose life took a rather unusual turn. It all began when he arrived at an emergency room one fateful morning, clutching his hand in agony. He claimed that a pygmy rattlesnake had bitten him, and the visible puncture marks and swelling on his hand seemed to support his story.

The medical team promptly sprang into action, administering antivenin, a potent snakebite antidote, along with narcotic pain medication. Joe's condition improved, and after some time, he was discharged, seemingly on the road to recovery.

However, fate had a different plan for Joe. Just a week later, he found himself in yet another emergency room, with a remarkably familiar tale of a rattlesnake bite. Once again, the medical staff treated him with antivenin and narcotic pain medication before sending him on his way. The Poison Center got both calls and found this unusual, two bites in a week.

The Poison Center, which provides guidance on managing venomous snakebites, received multiple calls from hospitals across five different counties, all seeking advice on how to handle this peculiar patient. As the episodes continued, Joe's desperation for narcotics became increasingly evident. In one visit, he claimed to have been bitten not only by a pygmy rattlesnake but also by a coral snake.

> **Patients often contact the Poison Center seeking help for drug addiction, highlighting a critical issue in our society.**

This claim raised eyebrows, as the two snakes were not typically found in the same area, and treating a coral snakebite was vastly different from treating rattlesnake bites. Narcotics are not given for coral snake bites because coral snake venom is a neurotoxin, and staying awake is crucial for monitoring and treatment. Joe miscalculated adding the coral snake bite to his exposure.

Joe was not associated with any wildlife-related work that might explain these snake encounters, and his true intentions became glaringly obvious.

The hospitals were made aware of the pattern and took measures to address the situation. The story of Joe serves as a stark reminder of the lengths to which some individuals may go to obtain narcotics.

Medication Mishaps

Prescriptions Gone Wild

A 21-year-old, who was prescribed 80 mg of Propranolol once a day, attempted to take her medication by tipping the bottle into her mouth, hoping that only one pill would come out. Unfortunately, this approach led to an accidental ingestion of an unknown quantity of the pills, resulting in a choking incident. This situation became a concern due to the uncertainty of the number of pills swallowed and the potential for adverse effects of overdose.

—

A five-year-old was able to climb up into a medicine cabinet in the bathroom where he found a full bottle of aspirin, 325 mg pills. Since it was a brand-new bottle, they determined the five-year-old could only have gotten one pill. The family counted the pills remaining in the bottle. One pill was not enough to send this child to the hospital. If there had been any question of how much aspirin the child could have gotten, he would have had to be treated in an emergency department.

—

There was a woman who usually used enemas once or twice a week due to her intestinal disease. She developed severe abdominal pain and rectal bleeding after getting an enema. It was found the saline bottle she usually used was on the counter. So was a bottle of 5% food-grade hydrogen peroxide, which she used by accident; it burned her intestines.

—

A young child cut his finger. His mother tried to do a little first-aid and grabbed a Band-Aid and some cream to put on the wound. What she thought was supposed to be an antibiotic cream unfortunately turned out to be a hemorrhoid cream. *Sometimes keeping all your medicines in one place can be a problem.*

After parents returned from a Caribbean cruise, they picked up their six-month-old baby from the child's grandparents. When they got the child home, they noticed the child had one excessively dilated pupil and was rubbing that eye.

Alarmed, they rushed the child to the emergency department to find out the cause. Although the baby was otherwise alert and playful, a closer examination and questioning revealed that the father had been wearing a Scopolamine patch behind his ear during the cruise to alleviate nausea. It turned out the child had touched the patch and then touched her eye, causing the dilation.

Fortunately, the solution was straightforward: Over time, the effects of the Scopolamine exposure would dissipate, and the pupil would return to its normal size. Until then dim lit rooms and/or sunglasses were necessary until the symptoms resolved.

—

It's not uncommon for people to mistakenly consume boric acid suppositories, often recommended for vaginal yeast infections. These suppositories are designed for vaginal insertion, not swallowing.

Fortunately, swallowing one suppository is typically not considered poisonous, and it's unlikely to cause significant harm. However, it will not be an effective treatment for the yeast infection when taken orally.

A wife called regarding her 80-year-old husband who had dementia. He had regular medicines that he took once a day. He took his medicine this morning. Accidentally, he took them again in the evening. It was his medications for hypertension and dementia. She was told by the poison specialist to watch him for dizziness, so she felt reassured. *On a follow-up call, he was fine and wanted to know if he could go for a walk. He was told, "sure, he could go for a walk." Then, he asked if he could lift weights...hopefully, he could lift weights before all of that.*

—

A 39-year-old woman arrived at the emergency room distressed because she accidentally used a Naproxen 500 mg pill instead of the morning-after pill. Her second mistake was placing the Naproxen pill in her vagina, while the morning-after pill is intended for oral ingestion. Although it was suggested that the Naproxen would not pose a major problem, it raises questions about whether the hospital checked to confirm if she was pregnant. A follow-up call later revealed that she was indeed pregnant.

—

A common scenario involves a respiratory medicine designed to have its capsule broken open, with the powder inside intended for inhalation. However, individuals accustomed to taking pills may inadvertently swallow the capsule instead of following the proper inhalation process. Fortunately, this is not poisonous, just a wasted medication since this medicine is not effective this way. In many cases, this mistake does not lead to significant problems.

Administering a new medication to a six-month-old baby with a recently diagnosed heart problem can be a cause for concern. In this case, the family was supposed to give the baby 0.7 mL of flecainide but received a 10 mL syringe from the pharmacy. Unknowingly, they administered 7 mL instead of the prescribed 0.7 mL of the drug. Flecainide has a narrow therapeutic window and can have life-threatening consequences if not administered correctly.

Upon realizing the error, they promptly sought medical attention at an emergency department. Thankfully, with medical support, the child tolerated the medication error well, highlighting the importance of quick medical intervention and monitoring in such situations.

—

While under the care of a babysitter, a five-year-old was meant to receive one clonidine pill, and the four-year-old was to receive half a pill. Due to some confusion, both children were given one and a half pills of clonidine. When the parents returned home, they found their children lethargic. These children were able to be watched at home by their parents with follow up by phone with the Poison Center.

—

A young man had been experiencing persistent coughing for the past 24 hours and attempted to alleviate it with cough medicine. He consumed a significant amount, approximately 4 ounces of the cough medicine, over the course of several hours. He contacted the Poison Center when he began having trouble standing, dizziness, and realized the bottle was empty. He wanted to know what else he could take.

> **He wanted to know what else he could take.**

A mother called, concerned that her two-year-old continued crying and shaking. They could not console the child. The mother thought she might have given the two-year-old the nine-year-old sibling's ADHD medicine, which could cause all those symptoms. The two-year-old was supposed to get an allergy pill. This child required emergency department evaluation.

—

The family called regarding a young teenager who had been on the same medicine for the last six months. Accidentally, this young lady took her medicine twice that morning. Since the child had been on the medicine for a while, it would likely not cause any significant harm.

—

A mother called with frustration. The father inadvertently gave their teenager a second dose of Adderall just 20 minutes after she had already administered the medication. She was concerned about this double dosage. While the situation was understandably distressing, she was reassured that the child would likely be fine.

—

In a hospital medical unit, a patient was being treated for elevated blood sugar levels and was meant to receive 10 units of fast-acting insulin. Unfortunately, due to an error, the patient received 100 units of insulin instead. Such an insulin overdose can lead to a significant drop in blood sugar levels. It was fortunate that the patient was in the hospital and was able to be monitored closely.

    A mother gave her one-year-old child an allergy medication before leaving for work. Unaware of this, the father later administered the same medication to the child. The mother only discovered the situation in the evening. The child did not experience significant issues throughout the day.

—

    A man called with concerns after experiencing hemorrhoid discomfort. Instead of applying hemorrhoid cream, he accidentally used Capsaicin muscle rub in the affected area. This resulted in intense burning when applied to sensitive areas like hemorrhoids. The recommended course of action was to thoroughly wash the affected area to remove the Capsaicin residue and alleviate the burning sensation.

—

    A man working the night shift in a factory took what he believed to be an allergy pill before his shift, only to realize later that it was his narcotic pain medication, which was causing extreme drowsiness and dizziness. He called seeking advice on how to counteract the effects so he could go to work.

—

    A concerned, adult woman called that she had taken one Melatonin tablet. She forgot and 30 minutes later took another one. Concerned that she would not wake up, Poison Control reassured her she would be safe.

A two-year-old was given 5 mL of liquid Methadone that belonged to the mother by mistake. Mom wanted to know if there was any treatment she could do at home. The child was supposed to get Ibuprofen not Methadone. Unfortunately, the child required support in the emergency department.

—

> **It was advised vomiting is not unusual, uncomfortable but not life threatening**

An elderly man called nauseated. He had vomited after drinking what he believed to be his Alka-Seltzer, mixing the tablets in the water. Unfortunately, the tablets that he mixed were denture cleaning ones. It was advised vomiting is not unusual, uncomfortable but not life threatening. He was fine.

—

A four-year-old was given allergy medicine by the mother. Thirty minutes later, her helpful grandmother repeated the dose. Well, it is not ideal for medication to be given by multiple caregivers. A double dose is unlikely to cause harm in most situations.

—

The family brought in a young woman who started taking St. John's Wort for an unknown reason. When she got to the emergency room, she was confused and agitated. The family asked, "Is this possibly a reaction to the St. John's Wort—and any other medicines that she is on?"

> **Sometimes you must ask enough questions to understand the situation.**

The father called a Poison Center. His concern was that his two-year-old had eaten some of the beads in a silica packet.

Upon further questioning, the silica packet was in a pill bottle of Wellbutrin 150 mg extended release (bupropion). The child was found with the bottle of pills spilled all over and the silica packet in the mouth.

The father initially doubted that the child had ingested pills but, upon further investigation, he took the child to an emergency department. It was crucial because they indeed found and removed five pills from the child's stomach. While the silica packet was not poisonous, it did pose a choking hazard. The pills themselves were toxic to the child.

Talk to an expert in the Poison Center

**National Poison Center
800-222-1222**

Toy vs Hazard

Child's Play Chaos

A parent allowed their eight-year-old child to play with a helium balloon in a restaurant where the child inhaled the helium gas. This seemingly harmless act took a dangerous turn when the child's eyes rolled back, and he lost consciousness, experiencing seizures. Fortunately, with the administration of oxygen, the child regained consciousness and recovered without lasting harm.

> This incident highlights the potential risks associated with inhaling helium. It can displace oxygen and lead to oxygen deprivation, resulting in health consequences such as loss of consciousness and seizures.

A seven-year-old was given a toy which included multiple small magnets. Swallowing a single magnet may not pose a significant problem but could be a choking hazard. However, if more than one magnet is swallowed, there is a risk that they may not travel together through the intestines and could cause an obstruction. In these situations, it is advisable to perform an x-ray, assess the location of the foreign objects, and remove them.

A four-year-old child removed magnets from the refrigerator and swallowed at least one, though the exact number was uncertain. An x-ray was performed, revealing only one magnet. Fortunately, the child passed the magnet in their stool without any issues, and no further complications were observed.

> **It is interesting how imaginative children can be when interpreting their experiences.**

In a follow-up call, the father humorously noted that the child had become cautious around the refrigerator, fearing that he might stick to it.

On the way home from the grocery store a mother and her seven-year-old stopped to get some gasoline. The child wanted to help pump gas. The mother got the gas pump all lined up and allowed the seven-year-old to hold the gas line. There was a back flash of gasoline that sprayed into the child's hair, eyes, and mouth.

A child's head is the perfect level for an accident.

A grandmother allowed her four-year-old to get out of the car while she pumped gas. She was very careful that he stayed close to her. Unfortunately, she lost control of the gas hose and gas backed out all over her legs and the child's head, face, and mouth.

The Terrible Two's

Aromatic Adventures

Bad things happen when the toddler gets up before the parents... A toddler was found in the laundry room while his parents were sleeping. He was eating lavender laundry beads and spitting them out.

—

A mother, while on the phone, looked over at her 18-month-old child. The child had taken apart the air freshener wick that was plugged in to the electrical socket and was sucking on it.

—

A teenager had gotten some vanilla scented, reed diffuser sticks and put them in her room. Unfortunately, her two-year-old brother got in there and was found sucking on them. If they smell good, surely, they must be good to taste.

—

In this incident, a grandmother called 911 and was subsequently connected to the Poison Center due to her concern that her two-year-old grandchild had ingested household bleach. The Poison Center advised her that, while bleach could be irritating, dilution with water or juice would likely alleviate the irritation. However, the child refused to drink anything at that moment.

Emergency Medical Services (EMS) arrived to assess the situation and found no apparent injury to the child's mouth. In a follow-up call, the grandmother reported that the child had only started drinking fluids once they arrived at the emergency room. She also mentioned that the child's behavior could be challenging at times, describing her as a "spoiled brat."

> **We make medications in chewable form and shaped like gummies so kids will eat them. Frequently if it tastes that good, they will figure out how to get more.**

A toddler got a container of deodorant. It smelled so good it must taste good. He was found spitting some out in the bathroom sink, evidence it was not too good to eat.

—

Singulair pills treat children with asthma. They are chewable and apparently quite tasty. A mother called about her five-year-old who had gotten the bottle of the Singular chewable pills. The child shared them with his two-year-old brother. The mother estimated that 12 to 15 pills were missing. Fortunately, there were no significant side effects from this.

—

This toddler was able to move a chair to the counter where he climbed up on the chair. He then proceeded onto the counter and then on top of the refrigerator—because guess where the gummy vitamins were?

Children can be motivated by treats and are capable of remarkable things—which can sometimes lead to dangerous situations. Young children have nothing else on their little minds, no mortgage or job, the mission critical for them was to get the tasty pills.

> **Never underestimate the determination of a toddler.**

Kids & Mayhem

A two-year-old child discovered a container of foot powder left out by a parent and proceeded to use it in a rather creative manner. The child ended up with powder in his hair, face, mouth, and all over his clothes. Additionally, the bedroom floor received a generous sprinkling. This child was supposed to be taking a nap. Despite the extensive powdering adventure, the child did not experience coughing or any severe adverse effects, ultimately surviving this powdery encounter.
Since all is well, perhaps another photo memory.

—

A two-year-old child was able to reach a tube of muscle rub. The curious toddler seized the opportunity and began chewing on the tube, breaking open the muscle rub into its mouth. The child screamed initially but was better after getting something to drink.

—

Teething tablets are another popular ingestion risk for young two-year-olds. They are itty-bitty, pills that come in small containers. Apparently, they're quite tasty. Children tolerate quite a few of these.

—

Children, left unattended in their cribs, may sometimes engage in exploratory behavior, including attempting to disassemble their diapers. In some cases, they may even try to ingest the materials found inside the diaper. *While this behavior can pose a choking hazard, this was more fun to play with than it was to eat. As a result, children typically do not consume large quantities from their diapers.*

A two-year-old accidentally ingested a swallow of 3% hydrogen peroxide that was accessible on the parents' bedside. In response to this ingestion, the child promptly vomited and quickly recovered.

—

Children, often in the process of having their diapers changed, may be able to grab the diaper rash cream to play with. Sometimes, they may get a taste of it. It would not be all that tasty. Most children will not make a meal of this. It may cause a greasy stool.

—

Gummy vitamins are tasty. I have had families tell me their toddler moved a chair to a counter to get to the top of a cabinet that contained the vitamins. Luckily, the gummy vitamins are generally safe and well tolerated. The containers they come in are "child resistant" not child proof. They are meant to slow children down but will not keep out determined or curious children.

> **Child-resistant caps on containers, while designed to slow children down, are not foolproof and should not replace vigilant supervision.**

There is no substitute for a parent's watchful eye when it comes to ensuring the safety of children in our homes. It's essential for adults to educate themselves about potential hazards, store items securely, and keep them out of reach of curious young ones.

Two-year-olds think Tums are tasty. A little antacid medication's rolls are frequently sitting out. If they are not in a child resistant container, they're tasty to a two-year-old who sucked on a bunch of those when given enough time alone.

—

During kitchen activities, it can be challenging for a mother to monitor a curious one-year-old who may be drawn to items like dishwasher detergent. Their cups are fascinating objects to explore. Sometimes, they dip their fingers into the detergent and get a taste of it.

—

A product that is in a lot of packaging is silica gel granules. They are used to keep things dry when products are shipped or stored. The little packets are cute and easy to get into. Little two-year-old's like to eat the little granules. They don't taste that good. Two-year-old's don't read the packaging that says, "do not eat". Years ago, the packaging used to have a skull and crossbones symbol on the package but not anymore. This is also a choking hazard.

> **Two-year-old's don't read the packaging that says, "do not eat."**

It's a critical reminder that many of us may not always take the time to read warning labels or fully understand the potential dangers associated with common items we have in our homes. Whether it's household products, medications, or even plants in our yards, awareness of these risks is crucial.

An eight-year-old was supposed to take a Depakote 500 mg pill, but a two-year-old sibling ingested the pill before him. It was important to seek guidance from the Poison Center as soon as possible. Following a consultation with the poison specialist, they determined that a single Depakote 500 mg pill should generally be tolerated well by the young child. This child was monitored at home. In many situations, there is no better vigilant person to monitor a child, than a parent.

> It is vitally important to store medications securely and out of reach of young children.

The following incident highlights the importance of keeping medications securely stored and out of reach of young children.

In this case, the two-year-old had access to the grandmother's medicine, which contained muscle relaxants. The child's mother was giving birth to another child in the hospital, and during that time, the toddler ingested the medication. This resulted in the child becoming unresponsive and requiring mechanical ventilation for some time. Fortunately, the child did recover from this incident.

"When children are in the care of grandparents, there are sometimes safety measures a parent would take that are not thought of by the grandparent."

Firework Fiascos

A toddler ingested a fireworks snake, also known as Pharaoh's snake, which transforms into a black powdery snake when ignited. Fortunately, the child did not choke on it, and it was determined not to be poisonous. Children's curiosity sometimes leads them to encounter spent fireworks or firecrackers and chew on them, like this situation. While such items can be unsettling to parents or caregivers, they are generally not considered toxic if ingested without choking.

—

> Glow sticks are a common product at many celebrations and are known to catch the attention of children.

Children, playing with these, take the glowing tubes in their mouths and bite down into them. They get the foul-smelling and, I have been told, nasty tasting liquid in their mouths. Kids usually start spitting it out after getting a taste. The taste is irritating, but are not poisonous.

—

However, I have had teenagers dare each other to drink the contents of the glow sticks. The contents caused them to vomit. Hopefully they learned a lesson about what dares they should act upon.

Any Container Will Do

Product Switcheroos

A young babysitter, looking after two children, aged three and four, noticed Kool-Aid in the refrigerator and served some to the children and herself. Shortly after, she began feeling dizzy. The three-year-old started shaking and hallucinating. Emergency Medical Services (EMS) were called. All three were taken to the hospital. Shockingly, it was later revealed that the parents had intentionally mixed Angel's Trumpet plants into the Kool-Aid to achieve a drug-induced high later.

Fortunately, the children and babysitter eventually recovered from the incident. Considering this alarming revelation, the Department of Children and Families was contacted to assess the children's home environment and safety.

—

During a barbecue, hosted by a man who owned a pesticide company, an unfortunate incident occurred involving one of his friends' three-year-old child. The child, in a moment of curiosity, found a juice bottle and started drinking from it. Shortly thereafter, the child began vomiting, leading to the discovery that the juice container had an organophosphate pesticide. The homeowner had apparently transferred the pesticide into the juice container with the intention of diluting it later.

Following this alarming discovery, the child underwent a lengthy treatment process but ultimately recovered from the pesticide exposure. This incident serves as a reminder about the critical importance of proper storage and labeling of any hazardous substance.

> **Let this be a reminder that accidents can happen, even with everyday tasks.**

A woman called with a rather unusual situation. While cleaning her floors and enjoying a cocktail, she accidentally picked up the cup containing floor-cleaning detergent instead of her cocktail, swallowing some of it. This mishap did lead to an upset stomach, but she managed to continue her cleaning after the incident.

—

A tragic incident occurred when a man returned home from golfing and, feeling thirsty, reached into the refrigerator for what he thought was a bottle of water. However, he had mistakenly grabbed a bottle containing 10% hydrogen peroxide, which his wife had inadvertently placed in the refrigerator.

After taking a sip, he immediately began foaming at the mouth. This man passed away because he had ingested concentrated hydrogen peroxide. This heartbreaking event serves as a stark reminder of the importance of proper storage and labeling of household chemicals to prevent such accidents from happening.

Properly stored and labeled household chemicals can prevent accidents from happening.

In another rather unfortunate mix-up, a family had borrowed laundry detergent from a friend, and stored it in a Gatorade bottle. Due to some confusion, this bottle ended up in the refrigerator. A four-year-old child, unaware of the content, accessed the refrigerator and began drinking from the Gatorade bottle, only to experience vomiting as a result. *It emphasizes the importance of storing household products in their original containers.*

Classroom Calamities

An emergency department was called regarding a nine-year-old who got some sunscreen in his eyes while at school. This can usually be flushed out readily, but apparently this child had difficulty with that process. When he arrived in the emergency department, he told the staff that the school nurse was a serial killer and was trying to kill him by drowning him. *Getting your eyes flushed with water can be uncomfortable.*

—

In a high school chemistry class, muriatic acid was used in an experiment. The container spilled on to one of the teenagers' hands. Irritation was the result..

Occupational Oopsies

A man, working at a construction site, accidentally got wet concrete into his boots. Instead of removing them immediately, he kept them on until he got home. By the time he took them off, he had damage to his skin. He had redness, pain, and blistering on his feet. The wet concrete caused a chemical burn. He needed to be evaluated by a burn specialist.

Anger Management

A teenager, upset after being grounded for staying out late, sought revenge by adding weed killer to her parents' vodka. However, the parents detected the unusual taste in their drinks and became suspicious. Upon questioning, the teenager admitted her actions.

—

A young woman, taking a shower suddenly began coughing and detected a foul odor upon stepping out. Unbeknownst to her, insect foggers had been activated in both the upstairs and downstairs areas of the house. She quickly sought fresh air outside to alleviate her discomfort.

Later, she learned that her boyfriend, angry with her, had set off insect foggers. They release pesticides in aerosol form to eliminate pests.

—

A caller reported a domestic dispute with her partner, which led to her partner moving out. Upon returning to her house, she noticed a strong pesticide odor.

She discovered that her partner had used an outdoor pesticide indoors. As a result, the caller experienced clothing that smelled of pesticide and developed a rash. She expressed concerns that her partner had poisoned her clothes. Given the potential legal implications of this situation, the caller was referred to law enforcement.

Pepper Spray—When Spice Meets Chaos

A family member got very upset because he couldn't watch his program on TV. He sprayed pepper spray throughout the house. It affected three of his children and his wife. They all developed respiratory irritation and coughing.

> The use of pepper spray in an indoor setting can release noxious fumes and irritants that can be harmful to anyone who was exposed.

A caller was in significant distress, sitting in a cool bath to alleviate the intense pain in her vaginal area. She couldn't urinate due to the pain. Her discomfort stemmed from an unusual source—she had a tampon in her purse that had been inadvertently exposed to pepper spray. This led to excruciating discomfort.

> "Pepper spray can have unintended and painful consequences when it meets sensitive areas of the body.
>
> Yikes, imagine..."

Random Calls

A caller had concerns about potential residues on his refurbished nose hair trimmer after rinsing it with water before use. He was unsure if any chemicals or contaminants might have remained on the trimmer. He was questioning if he got all the poisons off it?

—

A caller stated, "My neighbor does not like my dog and poisoned him. Where can I get the dog and the food tested for poisons?"

Another called asked, "If I burn something in the microwave, is it radioactive?"

"When lettuce turns brown is that rust?"

"I put sunscreen in my eyes so I could see the eclipse. Now I can't see, and my eyes hurt."

"I put sunscreen in my eyes so I could see the eclipse. Now I can't see, and my eyes hurt.

—

A mother discovered her two-year-old child coughing uncontrollably; the child drank from a glass containing vinegar. The child was able to drink water without difficulty... This was not poisonous but would be irritating. After drinking the water, the child felt better. When asked the child's name, the mother, said "God." *I asked her to spell it because I was not sure I heard her correctly. She spelled, "G-O-D."*

.A woman called expressing a concerning belief that the Secret Service was injecting heroin into her buttocks. She claimed that she had attempted to inform the police about this situation but was met with disbelief. The police had done nothing to help.

—

The father's concern stemmed from the belief that dollar bills are sometimes used for snorting cocaine. He was worried that his three-year-old child might have encountered cocaine residue while playing with the bill. *The father's concern for his child's safety was understandable; however, the likelihood of becoming exposed to cocaine, in this situation, was extremely low.*

—

The caller, who seemed disoriented, mentioned that he had entrusted some of his gold bars to a caretaker, but he wanted them back now. I am not sure who he was trying to reach.

—

Another caller expressed a concern about the taste of peach flavor in their nicotine vape pen. He wanted to know how to make the flavor stop.

One thought was to stop vaping. Another thought was, if he had Covid -19, he would not taste anything for a while. I decided not to make my inside voice suggestions.

One 30-year-old caller was experiencing COVID-19 symptoms and expressed concern about potential brain damage. He described a sensation about his brain shaking when he coughed. *This sensation is not indicative of brain damage but rather a result of the forceful coughing and the vibrations it can create in the head.*

—

A nursing home contacted the Poison Center about a 31-year-old developmentally delayed individual who had ingested an unspecified quantity of screws, bolts, and AAA batteries. Remarkably, the person exhibited no immediate symptoms of distress. However, upon conducting an x-ray in the emergency room, the foreign objects were in his stomach and subsequently removed.

—

A father called regarding his three-year-old who got 'parental' vitamins, not to be confused with prenatal vitamins. *The concern with prenatal vitamins is the potentially high iron content.*

—

When asking a family about the amount of liquid cough medicine their child consumed, the mother replied with "four Florida ounces (fl oz)." This humorous mix-up likely stemmed from a regional difference, as fluid ounces are the standard unit of measurement in most states.

> **A reminder that communication, especially in moments of concern, can sometimes lead to unexpected and amusing exchanges.**

> Where can I get tested for radiation poisoning? My ex-wife's cousin uses sound wave guns that create a pulsating whistling sound.
>
> Doesn't that make you have microwave burns?

"If I snort Elmer's glue, am I going to die?"

Why are you snorting Elmer's glue?

A family called regarding a young teenager who decided to pierce her belly button with a safety pin. Now, she has pain and brown drainage coming out. They were concerned about blood poisoning.

—

"If I snort Elmer's glue, am I going to die?" I asked, "Why are you snorting Elmer's glue?" The caller hung up.

—

"I'm hallucinating and my kidneys hurt. What should I do?"

—

A caller stated, "I shook the Worcestershire sauce and got some in my eye. Now, it's causing burning."

This patient got a corrosive cleaner in his eye. He then irrigated the eye very well with water. I asked him how his vision was. Usually, people say it's cleared up or it's not. This gentleman's description of his vision was, "It's like looking through lake water as opposed to looking through the blue Gulf of Mexico waters in the Keys."

—

"I was working out and got some sweat in my eyes. It was irritating so I flushed my eyes out with water, then I put some saline in them. I then flushed them with some milk. Do I need to do more?"

"My boyfriend got sperm in my eye.

What should I do?"

Now you know who to call, and when!

**National Poison Center
800-222-1222**

Is this number in your phone yet?

Conclusion

As I conclude this book, filled with poison stories, I hope you have laughed and gained valuable insights along the way. These tales, although often lighthearted, carry important lessons about safety and vigilance.

Remember, even in the most unexpected situations, knowledge can save lives. So, let's laugh at the absurdity of some of these moments, but also learn from them. I would like you to take away the message that accidents can happen to anyone, but with the right treatment, information, and quick action, we can treat many of them at home.

May these stories serve as a reminder to keep hazardous substances out of reach, read labels attentively, and stay informed about potential risks. I hope that you share these lessons with others, so they too can laugh, learn, and stay safe.

Thank you for joining me on this journey, and may your life be filled with both laughter and wisdom as you navigate the world of poisons.

National Helpline Phone Numbers

National Poison Centers
800-222-1222

USDA Meat and Poultry Hotline
800-535-4555

Butterball® Turkey Talk-Line®
800-BUTTERBALL, text 844-877-3456

National Suicide Hotline
800-273-8255 or call / text 988

ASPCA Animal Poison Center
888-426-4435
(this is not a free service)

National Sexual Assault Hotline
800-656-4673

National Domestic Violence hotline
800-228-0332

United States Elder Abuse Hotline
866-363-4276

National Child Abuse Hotline
800-422-4453

Disaster Distress Helpline
800-985-5990

> A poison specialist will ask When, How, Why, Where to help determine what happened then recommend the best treatment advice.

National Human Trafficking Hotline
888-373-7888

Rape, Abuse and Incest National Network
(RAINN)
800-656-HOPE (800-656-4613)

StrongHearts Native Helpline
844-7Native (844-762-8483)

Gay, Lesbian, Bisexual
and Transgender National Hotline
888-843-4564

Substance Abuse and
Mental Health Services Administration
(SAMHSA)
800-662-4357

Marijuana Anonymous
800-766-6779

Alcohol Treatment Referral Hotline
800-252-6465

About the Author

Charisse Webb, RN; CSPI, is a highly experienced registered nurse with a remarkable 42-year career. Her diverse roles include serving as a Certified Poison Information Specialist (CSPI), an Advanced Hazmat Life Support Instructor (AHLS), and a Critical Care Nurse. Throughout her extensive career, Charisse has gained expertise in various medical fields, including pediatrics, heart surgery, critical care, and toxicology. Her wide-ranging knowledge and skillset make her a valuable resource for handling health crises and addressing medical emergencies.

Beyond her professional life, Charisse enjoys a personal life shared with her videographer/producer spouse and their two loyal dogs who share their home.

Charisse's unique combination of professional expertise and storytelling skill ensures that her book provides readers with a captivating perspective on the challenges and experiences encountered by those working in the field of poison emergencies and healthcare.

Save this number in your telephone!

**Nationwide Emergency Poison Center
800-222-1222**

Charisse Webb RN; CSPI

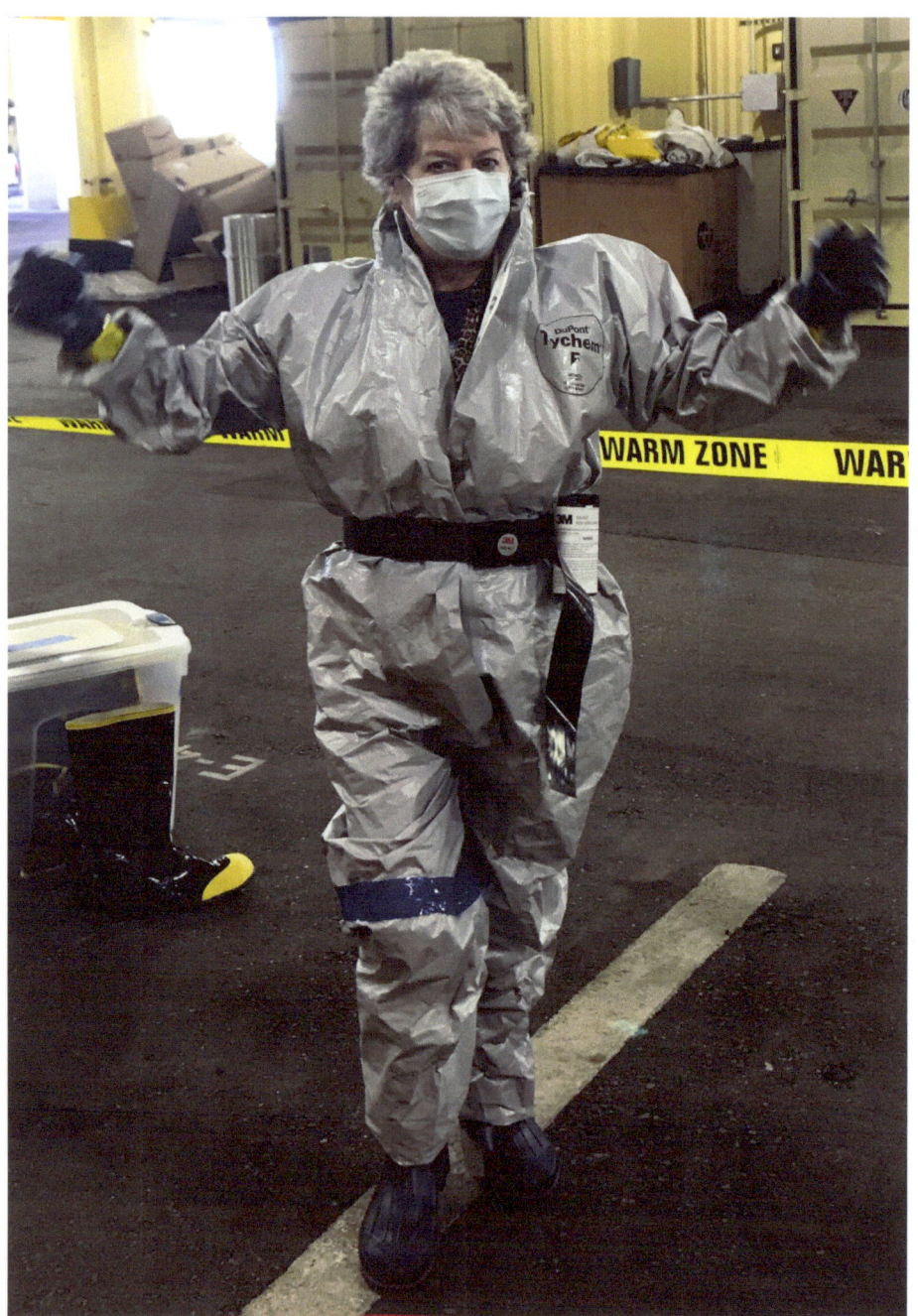

www.ingramcontent.com/pod-product-compliance
Lightning Source LLC
Chambersburg PA
CBHW042329150426
43193CB00005B/59